The WORLD
IN THE TIME OF
MARIE ANTOINETTE

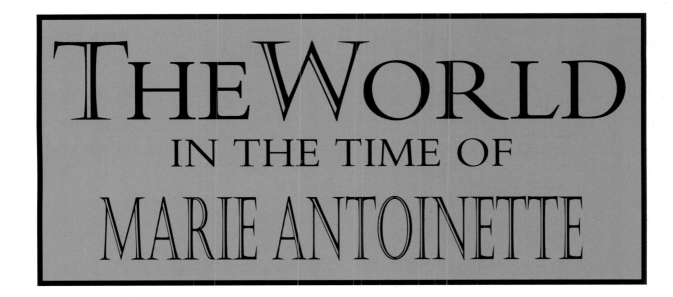

Belitha Press

F IONA M ACDONALD

First published in the UK in 1997 by

Belitha Press Limited, London House, Great Eastern Wharf,
Parkgate Road, London SW11 4NQ

Text by Fiona Macdonald
Map by Robin Carter, Wildlife Art Agency

ISBN 1 85561 708 0

British Library Cataloguing in Publication Data
for this book is available from the British Library.

Editor: Christine Hatt
Series Editor: Claire Edwards
Art Director: Helen James
Series Design: Roger Miller
Design: Jamie Asher
Picture Researcher: Diana Morris
Consultant: Sallie Purkis

Printed in Hong Kong
9 8 7 6 5 4 3 2 1

Picture acknowledgements:
AKG London: front cover r SMPK Kunstbibliothek Berlin; title page & 4; 5t
Akademie der Bilden Kuenste Vienna; 5b Palais de Versailles; 6b; 7t
Bibliothèque Nationale Paris; 13t Heeresgeschichtliches Museum Vienna; 13b;
18 Niederschsisches Landesmuseum Hannover; 19t Russian Museum St
Petersburg; 24; title page 28b Biblioteca del Palacio Real Madrid; 31t, 31b, 34.
Bridgeman Art Library: front cover c & 6t V & A Museum London; 7b
Giraudon/Musée de la Ville de Paris, Musée Carnavalet; 15b British Library; 16
Roy Miles Gallery, 29 Bruton Street, London W1; 17t National Library of
Australia Canberra; 22 Brooklyn Museum NY; 23b National Library of
Australia Canberra; 25b Christies London; 27t V & A Museum London; 27b
British Museum London; 28t Musée de la Co-operation Franco-Americaine; 29
Mitchell Library NSW; 30 NMM London; 36 Schloss Schonbrunn Vienna; 37t
The Hermitage St Petersburg; 37b Christies London; 40 Derby Museum & Art
Gallery; 41l Private Collection; 42 Museo Correr Venice; title page & 43b V &
A Museum London; 45 National Library of Australia Canberra.
Jean-Loup Charmet: 25t.

Corbis-Bettmann: 39.
ET Archive: 21b Musée Guimet Paris; 32t V & A Museum London; 33t; front
cover cl & 38r Marco Polo Gallery Paris; 41r Private Collection.
Werner Forman Archive: front cover l & 14 British Museum London; 15t;
contents & 20 Wallace Collection London; 35t Canterbury Museum
Christchurch; 38l British Museum London.
Robert Harding Picture Library: 21t, 44t.
Images of India: 43t Ilay Cooper.
National Maritime Museum London: 12.
Natural History Museum London: 35b.
Peter Newark's Pictures: 17b, 23t, 44b.
North Wind Picture Archive: 19b, 26.
Wellcome Centre Medical Photographic Library: 33b.

CONTENTS

ABOUT THIS BOOK

This book tells the story of Marie Antoinette, and looks at what was happening all around the world in her time. To help you find your way through the book, each chapter has been divided into seven sections. Each section describes a different part of the world, and is headed by a colour bar. As you look through a chapter, the colour bars tell you which areas you can read about in the text below. There is a time line, to give you an outline of world events in Marie Antoinette's time, and also a map, which shows some of the most important places mentioned in this book.

On page 46 there is a list of some of the peoples you will come across in this book. Some of the more unfamiliar words are also listed in the glossary.

THE STORY OF MARIE ANTOINETTE

► This glamorous portrait of Marie Antoinette was painted in 1778, when she had been Queen of France for four years. Marie Antoinette employed the top French designers, like Rose Bertin, to make her elaborate clothes. They set the fashion and were copied by noblewomen in many lands.

Queen Marie Antoinette lived in France just over 200 years ago. At the start of her life, she was surrounded by love and luxury – but she died a prisoner, hated by millions of ordinary people and deserted by most of her rich friends. This book will tell you about life in Marie Antoinette's France, and what was happening elsewhere in the world during Marie Antoinette's time. As Marie Antoinette's life was short – she died in 1793, aged only 37 – this book looks at a longer time span, from about 1700 to 1800. This will help you to find out more about the people, ideas and events that shaped the world Marie Antoinette knew, and to discover what happened in the years just after she died.

POWERFUL FAMILY

Archduchess Marie Antoinette Josephe Jeanne was born on 2 November 1755 into Europe's most powerful royal family. Her mother, Maria Theresa, was Empress of the Austrian Empire and ruled most of Central Europe. Her father, Francis I, was Duke of Lorraine, and also had the title Holy Roman Emperor. This gave him authority over many European kingdoms.

Marie Antoinette grew up in the royal palace in Vienna, the capital of Austria. She was not clever, but she was lively, pretty and fond of music, dancing, theatre and the other arts. From a young age, she was trained to be the wife of a great man. She learned how to present a good image in public and to be charming to visitors.

▲ Empress Maria Theresa of Austria with some of her many children on the terrace of the royal palace at Schönbrunn, near Vienna in Austria.

ARRANGED MARRIAGE

Queen Maria Theresa and Emperor Francis arranged marriages for their children. When Marie Antoinette was growing up, Maria Theresa wanted to make an alliance with France. So, in 1770, Marie Antoinette married Prince Louis, the young heir to the French throne. Louis was not interested in politics or economics, even though a successful ruler needed to understand both of these subjects. But in 1774, when he was 20, he was crowned King Louis XVI of France. Marie Antoinette, aged only 19, became queen.

▶ Prince Louis of France was tall, plump, shy, good-natured and dull. His main interests were hunting, food and metalwork.

FAMILY LIFE

Marie Antoinette found her husband and life at court boring. She spent most of her time with her friends and neglected her duties. The French began to say that she was a silly foreigner who spent too much. Her popularity increased after her first child was born in 1778. When two more babies followed, Louis was glad. He preferred family life to state affairs.

GOSSIP AND SCANDAL

It was not long before unfriendly gossip about Marie Antoinette started again. From 1784 to 1786, a scandal known as the Affair of the Diamond Necklace rocked France. Many people believed that Marie Antoinette had persuaded a priest to steal a diamond necklace for her, in return for promises of love. In fact, she was totally innocent, but the reputation of the royal family was still badly damaged.

Marie Antoinette spent her childhood surrounded by beautiful things. When she moved to France, she was delighted to find that French craftworkers were among the best in Europe, producing fine furniture, porcelain, silks and lace. This porcelain jug and bowl were made in the French factory of Sèvres in 1763. They are decorated in pure gold.

SERIOUS PROBLEMS

Even before Louis XVI became king in 1774, France faced serious problems. They grew worse during his reign. There were demands for changes in the way France was governed, a terrible financial crisis, and poverty and hunger in the countryside. Shut away in the palace, amusing herself with her elegant friends, Marie Antoinette did nothing to help. There was probably little she could have done, because her husband and his advisors did not want change. But her frivolous, expensive lifestyle angered many politicians and ordinary people throughout France.

REVOLUTION!

In 1789, the French people's anger exploded into a revolution. (You can read more about this on page 13.) In July, crowds attacked the Bastille, an ancient prison in the centre of Paris. Then, in October, they marched on the royal palace at Versailles, some distance from the capital. King Louis, Marie Antoinette and their three children were forced to move to an older, smaller palace in Paris itself. There they were kept under armed guard. To try to restore peace, King Louis agreed to all the protesters' demands. But he did not really intend to reform the government. At the same time, he allowed Marie Antoinette to write secretly to her family in Austria. She asked them for help to put an end to the French Revolution and to restore the royal family's power.

In October 1789, a mob of poor women market traders marched from Paris to attack the royal family in their palace at Versailles. After a year of economic crisis and serious shortages of food, they demanded bread to feed their families, and lower taxes.

▲ King Louis and Queen Marie Antoinette were recognized as they tried to escape, and soldiers loyal to the revolution took them prisoner.

ESCAPE ATTEMPT

In 1791, King Louis, Marie Antoinette and their children disguised themselves in servants' clothes and escaped from the palace at night. They hurried towards Belgium, where Marie Antoinette's brother was waiting with an army, ready to rescue them. But their bid to win freedom failed. Just a few kilometres away from the border, King Louis was recognized by a local postmaster, who had seen his portrait on banknotes. The king and his family were arrested and taken back to a Paris prison in disgrace.

▶ The guillotine was designed as a humane alternative to hanging. But during the French Revolution it proved to be a deadly machine for mass executions. It was used to kill not only the king and queen, but also thousands of nobles, priests and supporters of the royal family.

VICTIMS OF THE GUILLOTINE

Early in 1792, the Austrians invaded France. They wanted to put an end to the revolution and free Louis and Marie Antoinette. But they were forced to retreat. In August, the leaders of the revolution declared that the king and queen no longer had the right to rule, and that France was to become a republic. In December, Louis was tried for 'crimes against the state'. He was found guilty and publicly guillotined on 21 January 1793.

Marie Antoinette remained in prison for a few months more. But soon she, too, was put on trial. Revolutionary leaders accused her of treason. They said that she had plotted secretly against the revolution and encouraged the Austrians, who were enemies of France. They found her guilty and sentenced her to death. She was eventually executed by guillotine on 16 October 1793.

THE WORLD 1700-1800

ABOUT THE MAPS

The maps on this page will help you find your way around the world in Marie Antoinette's time. The big map shows some of the places mentioned in the text, including:

• **COUNTRIES** that are different from modern ones, such as Persia, as well as some important states and regions.

• *Past peoples*, such as the Seneca. The descendants of these peoples often live in the same place today, but their traditional lifestyles have almost vanished.

• *GEOGRAPHICAL FEATURES*, including mountains and rivers.

• *Towns and cities.* To find the position of a town or city, look for the name in the list below then find the number on the map.

1	Williamsburg	8	Istanbul	15	Rangoon
2	Montreal	9	Djenne	16	Bangkok
3	Quebec	10	Timbuktu	17	Penang
4	Bath	11	Amritsar	18	Qufu
5	Paris	12	Jaipur	19	Canton
6	Vienna	13	Delhi	20	Nagasaki
7	St Petersburg	14	Calcutta		

The little map shows the world divided into seven regions. The people who lived there were linked by customs, traditions, beliefs, or simply by their environment. There were many differences within each region, but the people living there had more in common with each other than with people elsewhere. Each region is shown in a different colour – the same colours are used in the headings throughout the book.

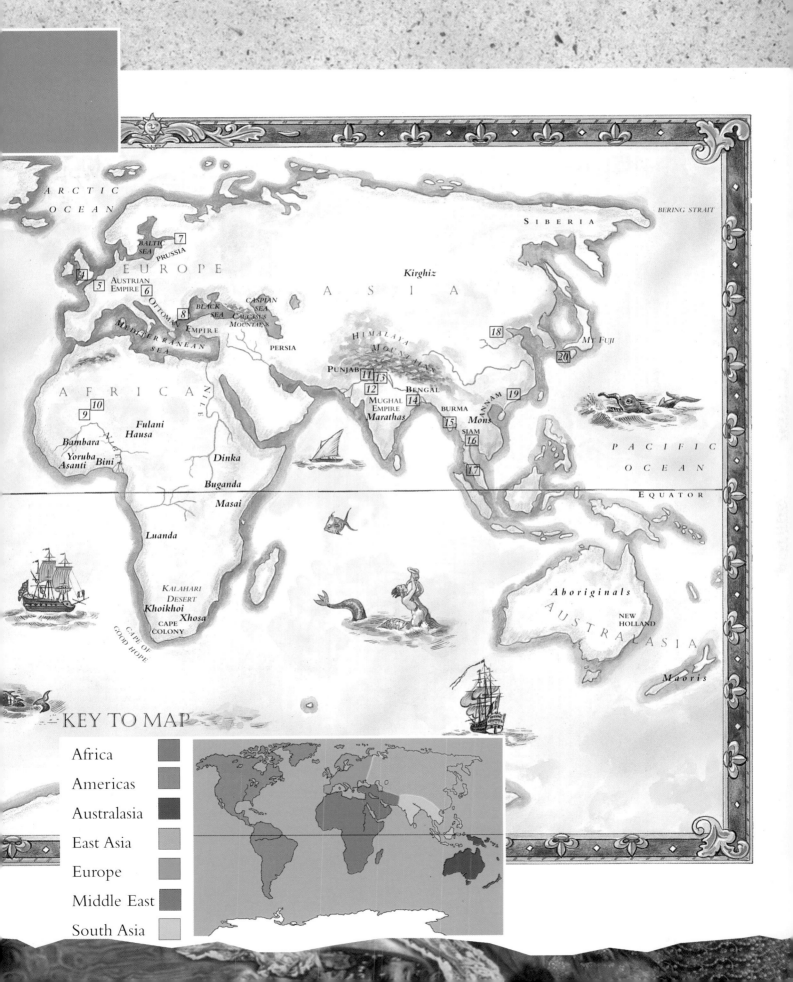

ARCTIC
OCEAN

SIBERIA

BERING STRAIT

BALTIC
SEA
7
PRUSSIA

E U R O P E

Kirghiz

A S I A

4

5

AUSTRIAN
EMPIRE
6

CASPIAN
SEA

CAUCASES
MOUNTAINS

OTTOMAN

BLACK
SEA

8

EMPIRE

18

MT FUJI

MEDITERRANEAN

SEA

PERSIA

20

HIMALAYA
MOUNTAINS

PUNJAB

AFRICA

NILE

11 13

12

MUGHAL
EMPIRE
Marathas

14

BENGAL

BURMA

ANNAM

19

10

9

Fulani
Hausa

Bambara

Yoruba
Asanti Bini

Dinka

Buganda

15

16

Mons

SIAM

PACIFIC

OCEAN

17

EQUATOR

Masai

Luanda

KALAHARI
DESERT

Khoikhoi

Xhosa

CAPE
COLONY

CAPE OF
GOOD HOPE

Aboriginals

AUSTRALASIA

NEW
HOLLAND

Maoris

KEY TO MAP

Africa

Americas

Australasia

East Asia

Europe

Middle East

South Asia

TIME LINE

1700   **1725**

EUROPE

1702 First English-language daily newspaper, *The Daily Courant*, published in London.

1700–1721 Russia and Sweden fight Great Northern War for control of far north of Europe.

1703 Peter the Great of Russia founds St Petersburg.

1707 England and Scotland unite to form Great Britain.

1701–1713 War of the Spanish Succession

1715 First Jacobite rebellion in Scotland. Supporters of Stuart dynasty oppose new British ruling family, the Hanoverians.

1718 German Gabriel Fahrenheit invents mercury-filled thermometer.

1727 British mathematician and astronomer Sir Isaac Newton dies, aged 85.

1740–1786 Frederick the Great rules Prussia.

1735 Swedish scientist Carolus Linnaeus invents a new system of classifying plants and animals.

1745 Second Jacobite rebellion in Scotland.

MIDDLE EAST

1722–1774 War between Ottoman Turkey and Russia.

1729–1732 War between Persians and Afghans.

c.1735 Wahhabi religious reform movement begins in Arabia.

1736–1747 Reign of Nadir Shah in Persia.

1737–1747 Persians invade Afghanistan.

AFRICA

1700 Asanti kingdom becomes powerful in West Africa.

1705 Tunis wins independence from Ottoman rule.

1710 Algeria wins independence from Ottoman rule.

1711 Tripoli wins independence from Ottoman rule.

1730 Kingdom of Borno becomes powerful in Sudan.

1747–1748 Yoruba people of Nigeria conquer nearby Dahomey and Benin.

SOUTH ASIA

1711 Dutch settlers in East Indies begin to set up coffee plantations.

1707 Mughal Empire begins to collapse after death of Emperor Aurangzeb.

1714 Maratha princes begin to become powerful in central India.

1739 Persian ruler Nadir Shah attacks city of Delhi.

EAST ASIA

1715 China conquers Mongolia.

1720 China conquers Tibet.

1703 Over 200,000 people die in Japanese earthquake.

1736–1796 Reign of Chinese emperor Qianlong.

AMERICAS

1701 Peace treaty between French settlers and Native Americans in north-east America.

1714–1716 War between French settlers and Native Americans.

1728–1733 Dane Vitus Bering explores Alaska.

1738 George Whitefield begins Great Awakening religious movement in North America.

1744–1748 King George's War between French and English settlers in North America.

AUSTRALASIA

1699–1701 British explorer William Dampier travels along coastline of Australia and Papua New Guinea.

1721–1722 Dutch explorer Jacob Roggeveen travels to Samoa, the Solomon Islands and Easter Island.

1750　　　　　　　　　　　**1775**　　　　　　　　　　　**1800**

1751–1777 French scholar Denis Diderot publishes his Encyclopedia.

1755 Marie Antoinette born.

1756–1763 Seven Years' War

1762–1796 Catherine the Great rules Russia.

1767 British inventor James Hargreaves makes 'spinning jenny' machine to spin woollen thread.

1773 Cossack rebellion led by Pugachev in Russia.

1775 Scottish scientist James Watt invents steam engine.

1789 French Revolution begins.

1790 Italian doctor Luigi Galvani investigates electricity.

1793 Queen Marie Antoinette and King Louis XVI executed.

1799 Army general Napoleon seizes power in France.

1763 Wahhabi religious leaders begin to take control of Arabia.

1770 Scottish explorer James Bruce reaches source of Blue Nile River.

1776–1786 Fulani people set up Muslim states in West Africa.

1779–1781 and 1793 Wars between Xhosa people of southern Africa and Boer (Dutch) settlers.

1789–1791 Russia conquers all Ottoman lands to north of Black Sea.

1793 Sultan Selim III reforms Ottoman Empire.

1799 French army general Napoleon invades Holy Land.

1790 Buganda kingdom expands in East Africa.

1795 British troops occupy Cape of Good Hope.

1798 Napoleon invades Egypt.

1755–1756 King Alaungpaya begins to unite Burma and founds Rangoon.

1757 Britain defeats troops from Bengal at Battle of Plassey.

1758 Marathas capture Punjab.

1782 Rama I becomes king of Siam.

1786 Britain gains control of Singapore, Malacca and Penang.

1767–1769 China invades Burma and demands tribute.

1775 Chinese population reaches 264 million.

1791–1792 War between China and Tibet.

1793 Chinese refuse British request to trade.

1751 Benjamin Franklin's experiments with electricity.

1759 Britain captures Quebec in Canada and lands west of the Mississippi River from France, and Florida from Spanish.

1763 Britain wins control of Canada.

1776 American Declaration of Independence

1780–1782 Revolt led by Tupac Amaru against Spanish in Peru.

1783 Peace treaty ends American War of Independence.

1789 George Washington becomes first President of USA.

1791 Revolt by slaves in Haiti led by Toussaint L'Ouverture.

1793 Eli Whitney invents cotton gin.

1769 Captain Cook reaches New Zealand.

1770 Captain Cook claims New Holland (New South Wales in Australia) for Britain.

1779 Captain Cook killed in Hawaii.

1788 Britain transports first convicts to Australia.

1793 First free settlers arrive in Australia.

Many of the dates shown in this Time Line are approximate. The letter c. stands for the Latin word circa, and means 'about'.

AROUND THE WORLD

The world changed dramatically between 1700 and 1800. Kings and queens, like Louis XVI and Marie Antoinette, were toppled from their thrones, and conquered peoples and colonies began to demand the right to govern themselves. Bigger ships, better navigation techniques and a new spirit of curiosity led to more contacts between countries. Most links were made through trade. This was sometimes of a shameful sort, particularly when millions of Africans were transported across the Atlantic Ocean as slaves. Meanwhile, European soldiers, missionaries and explorers began to spread European power around the globe.

▲ East Indiamen were cargo ships that sailed between Europe and the Far East. Cotton, sugar and other exotic goods from Asia and the Americas were rarely found in Europe in 1700. But by 1800, thanks to ships like these, they could be bought there quite cheaply and easily.

CONSTANT WARFARE

EUROPE

Throughout the 1700s, many nations in Europe were almost constantly at war. Austria, France and Prussia were the strongest and richest. When one of them grew too strong and threatened to take control of Europe, the other two fought against it together. This was called 'keeping the balance of power'. Smaller nations often got involved in the fighting, too. In northern Europe, there was a similar struggle between Sweden and Russia for control of the countries around the Baltic Sea.

▲ This flag was carried by Prussian soldiers during the Seven Years' War (1756–1763) against Austria and France. The Latin motto in the centre means 'For glory and homeland'.

THE FRENCH REVOLUTION

France faced many problems when Marie Antoinette was queen (see pages 4–7). By 1789, King Louis XVI's failure to find solutions led to a revolution. The leaders of the revolution wanted to end poverty and hunger, and to introduce fair government. From September 1793 to July 1794, extremists like lawyer Maximilien Robespierre organized a Reign of Terror, in which about 15,000 'enemies of the revolution' were guillotined. After the king and queen were executed in 1793, revolutionary leaders tried to spread their ideas of liberty and equality by conquering other European lands. So their rulers declared war on France and refused to buy French goods. The commander of the French army was Napoleon Bonaparte, and in 1799 he took over the government of France, too.

OTTOMAN DEFEAT

MIDDLE EAST

Terrible wars were also fought in many Middle Eastern countries. Between 1722 and 1774, Russia and the powerful Ottoman sultans of Turkey fought three times for control of territory around the Black and Caspian Seas. In 1774, Russia defeated the Ottomans. Most Russian harbours were blocked by ice in winter, but this victory gave them access to warm-water ports on the Black Sea that did not freeze over. The Russian Orthodox Church – closely linked to the Russian government – also gained the right to represent Christians living in Ottoman lands.

AFGHANS AND PERSIANS

From 1722 to 1730, Afghan troops occupied the neighbouring country of Persia (present-day Iran). In 1732, the Persians managed to drive them out. Then, led by new ruler Nadir Shah (see page 19), they captured Iraq and parts of Russia. In 1739, the Persians successfully invaded India, conquering much of the north and west.

▼ Russian soldiers defeating the Turkish army at the Battle of Kagul in 1770.

GREAT EMPIRES

West Africa was home to many great empires during the 1700s – the Asanti of present-day Ghana, the Bambara of Nigeria, and the Yoruba of Dahomey and Benin. They all grew rich through trading in gold, metalwork, ivory and slaves. Further to the south, the Luanda people founded a kingdom in the rainforests of Central Africa. In south-east Africa, the hunting and cattle-herding Masai people expanded their control over a vast area of savannah land. In and around the region of present-day Uganda, the Buganda kingdom also seized control of new territories.

▲ Magnificent gold jewellery, decorated with leaves and flowers, was worn by senior government officials at the Asanti kings' court. Many African kingdoms grew rich through trading in gold.

THE SLAVE TRADE

A form of slavery had existed in many parts of Africa for thousands of years. Most slaves in these traditional societies were either criminals or prisoners-of-war. But by 1750, the old laws regulating slavery had been swept away. European merchants demanded at least 60,000 slaves a year from traders in West Africa. Families, even whole villages, were rounded up and marched to the coast. Lives were wrecked and communities destroyed. Historians estimate that between 6 and 7 million African men, women and children were transported across the Atlantic Ocean between 1700 and 1800 to work as slaves in the Americas.

COLONY ON THE CAPE

In 1652, Jan van Riebeeck and some other Dutch farmers had founded the first European colony on the Cape of Good Hope, at the tip of southern Africa. By 1700 their descendants were beginning to explore further inland. They settled in sheltered, fertile river valleys, planted vineyards and ran cattle farms. In 1795, British troops captured the Cape Colony from the Dutch.

MUGHALS IN DECLINE

Ever since 1526, the magnificent Mughal dynasty of Muslim emperors had ruled India. But by the 1700s, Mughal power was fading. European merchant companies – especially those run by the British and French – controlled the most profitable parts of Indian trade, together with large areas of Indian land. Local Indian princes, such as the Marathas of central India and the Sikhs of the Punjab region in the north, took advantage of the Mughals' weakness to set up kingdoms of their own. India was also invaded twice in the eighteenth century, by the Persians in 1739, and the Afghans in 1761.

◀ Forts like this were built to house the many European merchants who traded along the west coast of Africa, and to store valuable 'goods', including slaves.

EUROPEANS IN INDIA

The British and the French were rivals in India. Troops of the British East India Company, led by an ambitious young businessman, Robert Clive, defeated the French army in a series of battles between 1751 and 1763.

British soldiers also fought against local Indian princes. In 1756, the Nawab (ruler) of Bengal, the richest region of India, imprisoned 146 British people in a tiny dungeon. Many died of suffocation. British people in India were outraged, and the prison became known as the Black Hole of Calcutta. In 1757, Clive and his troops defeated the Nawab at the Battle of Plassey, and Bengal came under British control.

Between 1775 and 1782, Britain and the Maratha princes were also at war. But the East India Company used peaceful negotiations to win the right to collect taxes on behalf of the Mughal emperors in many other Indian states.

EXPANSION OF TRADE

The British East India Company was not active in India alone. In 1700, it established a trading post in Borneo (in present-day Indonesia), and in 1786 built a larger trading settlement in Penang, Malaysia. Company members were keen to make profits from Asian spices, jewels and drugs.

▶ This scene from 1790 shows John Mowbray, a British East India Company merchant, in his office with his financial advisor.

▲ European and American offices and warehouses flying their national flags in the Chinese port of Canton.

CHINESE POWER

EAST ASIA

In 1700, China was the strongest nation in East Asia, and by 1800 had increased in power. Chinese emperors invaded Mongolia in 1715 and Tibet in 1720, and forced other lands to pay them tribute (see page 21). They also tried to control Europeans on Chinese territory, to prevent them introducing dangerous new ideas. From 1757, Europeans were allowed to live and work only in the port of Canton. Wars made China powerful, but trade and industry made China rich. Silk, porcelain and paper were made there and exported around the world.

A CLOSED NATION

Like the Chinese emperors, the rulers of Japan did not want foreigners to enter their land. So from 1639 to 1853, they closed the nation to them, allowing only a few Dutch and Chinese traders into Nagasaki port. But trade continued. Every year, Japan exchanged thousands of tonnes of silver for Chinese silk to weave into kimonos.

COLONIZATION

AMERICAS

At the beginning of the 1700s, North and South America were ruled as colonies by various European states. England and France controlled settlements in the region of present-day Canada and the USA, while Spain and Portugal 'owned' Central and South America. Several different European nations claimed the various islands of the Caribbean Sea.

DANGEROUS LIFE

By 1700, large areas of eastern North America, and the accessible parts of South America, had long been settled and farmed by Europeans eager to make their fortunes. The settlers faced a variety of dangers, including the harsh climate, poisonous wildlife and Native Americans furious at being turned off their ancient homelands. European settlers from different colonies became rivals, too. From 1744 to 1748, and again from 1756 to 1763, the British and French fought against one another on American soil.

COLONIAL WARS

In 1759, the British captured the important city of Quebec from France. The next year, they captured Montreal and gained control of the Great Lakes region and the St Lawrence River. French and British armies encouraged rival Native American peoples to fight alongside their troops. This led to bitter quarrels among Native American leaders, and bloodshed among both Americans and Europeans.

AMERICAN INDEPENDENCE

More fighting followed after the 13 British colonies in North America broke away from British rule. They were angry at having to pay British taxes, disagreed with Britain's policies in Canada, and wanted to govern their country as they chose. War broke out in 1775, and in July 1776, the Americans signed a Declaration of Independence. But fighting continued until 1781, when the British surrendered. In 1783, Britain recognized the 13 colonies as an independent nation – the United States of America. In 1789, George Washington, leader of the American army, was chosen as the first president of the USA.

▲ This picture shows explorer Captain Cook claiming possession of eastern Australia on behalf of the British government in 1770.

SOUTHERN CONTINENT

AUSTRALASIA

By 1700, Pacific sailors had already been travelling amazing distances between remote islands for centuries. So the vast region of Australasia was far from unknown to them. But it was not well-known to Europeans, the most powerful people in the eighteenth-century world.

European geographers had long suspected that a great Southern Continent might exist. But they did not know for sure until eighteenth-century adventurers brought back news of Pacific island peoples, animals and plants (see page 35). In 1770, during his first Pacific voyage, British explorer Captain James Cook landed on this continent – Australia – and claimed part of it, New Holland (now New South Wales), for Britain. The British government transported the first settlers, who were convicts, there in 1788.

◄ The American Declaration of Independence was signed on 4 July 1776. It began with the ringing words: 'We hold these truths to be self-evident, that all men are created equal...'

FAMOUS RULERS AND LEADERS

In the time of Marie Antoinette, people in many parts of the world began to ask questions about how they should be governed. Who had the right to rule? Were kings and queens appointed by God? Should they inherit their role? Or should they be chosen by ordinary people? Did every country have the right to govern itself? Or did powerful nations have the right to colonize or occupy other countries? And what about laws? Should they be based on religious beliefs, ancient traditions, or decisions made in parliaments elected by the people? All these questions were fiercely discussed in the 1700s. But different rulers and leaders had different ideas about how they should be answered.

◄ King Frederick the Great of Prussia (ruled 1740–1786) was a brilliant army commander. He made Prussia the second most powerful state in Europe, after its rival, Austria.

◀ Empress Catherine the Great of Russia (ruled 1762–1796) was a remarkable woman. At home, she punished her critics harshly. Abroad, she led successful army campaigns, conquering new territory and making Russia rich and strong.

NADIR SHAH

MIDDLE EAST

Nadir Shah of Persia was born in 1688, the son of a chieftain in the wild frontier lands between Persia and Afghanistan. He won fame as a brilliant cavalry officer, fighting alongside the Persians to drive out Afghan armies from their land. By 1732, when the Afghans were defeated, Nadir Shah controlled all Persia. The king, Abbas III, was still a baby, so Nadir Shah made himself regent and ruled in his place. He captured Iraq from the Ottomans in 1733, then conquered Russian land in the Caucasus Mountains. In 1736, he deposed Abbas and declared himself king. In 1739, he invaded India, occupied the capital city of Delhi, and seized vast amounts of treasure from its Mughal palaces.

ROYAL RULERS

EUROPE

Marie Antoinette's parents in Austria and her husband's family in France, Frederick the Great of Prussia and Catherine the Great of Russia, were all typical European rulers of the 1700s. They believed that they had the absolute right to govern their countries, and that people should obey them without question.

These monarchs took all power into their own hands and ignored the advice of assemblies of nobles and wealthy citizens. Instead, they appointed their own advisors and government officials, and often controlled the army, too. They also kept magnificent courts and held ceremonies that displayed their power. Some of these rulers did introduce social and educational reforms. But their refusal to let people share in government led to trouble and, in France, to revolution.

▶ Nadir Shah, ruler of Persia, was successful, but totally ruthless. Anyone who disagreed with him was killed. In 1747, he was assassinated by religious leaders and army officers who could stand his terrible cruelty no longer.

OTTOMAN EMPIRE

MIDDLE EAST

During the 1700s, the rulers of the Ottoman Turks had to battle against enemies within and outside their empire. Sultan Ahmed III (ruled 1703–1730) spent the early years of his reign fighting the Russians. The war ended in 1711, when the Ottomans won. But Ahmed's next war, against Austria, ended in Turkish surrender. In 1730, after Persian ruler Nadir Shah had conquered a large area of Ottoman land, Ahmed was removed from power by the Janissaries, an elite regiment in his army. He died six years later.

Sultan Selim III (ruled 1789–1807) fought Russia, Great Britain and powerful warlords in his own lands before he, too, was overthrown by the Janissaries. In 1807 they put him in prison, where he was murdered the next year.

CITY-STATES AND KINGDOMS

AFRICA

During the 1700s West Africa was divided into many kingdoms and city-states, home to peoples such as the Hausa, the Yoruba, the Fulani and the Bini. They were governed by powerful rulers, such as Usman dan Fodio (1754–1817), whose Fulani people conquered the Hausa lands in northern Nigeria. He and his followers were Muslims, and set up an empire ruled by Muslim laws (see page 42).

A little further south, the Bini people of Benin were led by rich kings called obas. Akenzua I, Eresoyen and Akengbuda were also strong warriors, and keen to encourage trade in goods such as pepper, ivory and fine brass work. Towards the end of Akengbuda's reign, his power faded, and Benin was weakened by civil wars.

INDIAN KINGDOMS

SOUTH ASIA

At this time, large areas of India were controlled by British and French trading companies, but there were also many independent kingdoms, ruled by princes, peshwas (chief ministers) and religious leaders. These kingdoms sometimes fought among themselves, and often clashed with the British. Hyder Ali became ruler of Mysore in southern India around 1760, after winning fame as a daring warrior. He conquered many nearby lands, but was defeated by the British in 1781, and died the next year. Hyder Ali's son, Tippu Sultan (ruled 1782–1799), continued his struggle.

◄ This gold head was made to decorate a royal stool used by Asanti obas (kings) in West Africa. It is probably a portrait of an enemy ruler killed in battle.

▲ Gold monkey statues and curving roofs decorate Bangkok's Grand Palace. The palace was built for King Rama I.

BURMA AND SIAM

In 1752, Prince Alaungpaya of Burma defeated the Mons people, who had invaded the northern half of the country. In 1755, he established a new capital city at Rangoon, and a year later won control of all Burma. He then became king, founding a new dynasty. In 1782, Chao Phraya Chakri became King of Siam (modern Thailand), taking the title Rama I. He made Bangkok the country's capital and built the Grand Palace and the Temple of the Emerald Buddha at its heart.

▼ Ambassadors from the Kirghiz people of far western China bringing valuable horses to present to Emperor Qianlong as tribute.

EMPEROR QIANLONG

EAST ASIA

During the reign of Emperor Qianlong (ruled 1736–1796), China was rich and powerful, with a strong army, harsh laws and a vast government bureaucracy. Qianlong's armies forced other East Asian states, including Korea, Burma and Annam (present-day Vietnam) to pay tribute.

Like earlier Chinese rulers, Qianlong believed that China was a special 'Middle Kingdom' at the centre of the world, and that Chinese civilization was better than any other. In 1793, the British government sent Lord McCartney to China, to investigate possibilities for trade. But Qianlong refused to consider trade links. He said that China did not need to buy anything from elsewhere.

Qianlong ruled for 60 years, then retired. He did not think it right to reign for longer than his famous grandfather, Emperor Kanxi (ruled 1661–1722). But many people, both in China and outside, thought that Qianlong had been in power for too long. By the end of his reign, the government was short of money, its officials were inefficient, and the army was run down. The population was growing rapidly, and there were also food shortages in many parts of the empire.

GEORGE WASHINGTON

AMERICAS

George Washington (1732–1799), the USA's first president, was born into a wealthy, upper-class family. They lived in Virginia, a British colony on the east coast of North America. Washington began his career as a soldier, fighting for the British against French soldiers and settlers in the wars for control of American lands (see pages 16-17). By the age of 23 he had been promoted to the rank of colonel and appointed commander of Virginia's colonial troops. Next, he went into politics. By 1769 he was leading the growing opposition of American settlers to British colonial rule. Like many other Europeans living in America, George Washington wanted independence for his country.

THE AMERICAN REVOLUTION

When the American Revolution broke out in 1775, Washington was chosen to lead the revolutionary army. He won great praise as a leader, and for his quick thinking on the battlefield. After Britain was defeated, Washington retired for a while to his family estate at Mount Vernon, where he concentrated on farming, breeding horses and dogs, gardening and business ventures. In 1787, together with other famous politicians such as Benjamin Franklin, he took part in the discussions about the constitution for the newly independent USA. In 1789, he was unanimously elected president. By the time he died, ten years later, he was widely respected as 'the Father of his Country'.

▲ George Washington, the first president of the USA, shown with two symbols of his brilliant career. These are a sword, to show his success in battle, and a pen, to show that he helped to write the laws of the new country that he governed.

RESISTANCE AND REBELLION

In North America, Native American leaders such as Cornplanter (died 1836), chief of the Seneca, and Pontiac (about 1720–1769), chief of the Ottawas, fought against Europeans who had settled on their homelands. In South America, Tupac Amaru, a descendant of the great Inca emperors who had once ruled Peru, led a rebellion against Spanish settlers from 1780 to 1782. On the Caribbean island of Haiti, a slave called Toussaint L'Ouverture (1743–1803) led a rebellion against the French in the 1790s. He and his followers demanded an end to slavery, and freedom to run their country by themselves. They were supported by a group of French thinkers called *Les Amis des Noirs* (Friends of Black People). Toussaint was captured and taken to France, where he died in prison in 1803. But Haiti was granted independence the next year.

▼ Cornplanter, leader of the Native American Seneca people of the north-eastern USA, painted in 1796. The artist has shown him wearing a feathered headdress and carrying a ceremonial tobacco pipe.

▲ A chief and two warriors from Hawaii, in the Pacific Ocean, as painted by a European artist who travelled there in 1787.

HAWAIIAN ISLANDS  AUSTRALASIA

In the Pacific, King Kamehameha I (1758–1819) conquered most of the Hawaiian islands and founded a new dynasty. The next four kings all had his name. King Kamehameha introduced new laws, fought against crime and encouraged trade. He was interested to meet foreign sailors and explorers who visited Hawaii, and was impressed by European technology. But he insisted on preserving Hawaii's ancient customs and traditional religious beliefs. He upheld the ancient system of taboos – laws that prohibited certain activities and relationships – and refused to let Christian missionaries land.

HOW PEOPLE LIVED

In some ways, life in Marie Antoinette's time was much as it had been for hundreds of years. Food was still produced by farm labourers and most craft goods were still made by hand. There was still a great difference between the living standards of the wealthy few and of the ordinary masses, who were miserably poor. But there were also changes. The growth of international trade meant that foreign goods and ideas were spreading all around the world. European families wore Indian cotton. They drank hot chocolate made from American cocoa, sweetened with Caribbean sugar. Native Americans rode European horses, and killed their prey with European knives. West African armies carried Portuguese muskets. By 1792, British sailors and traders were travelling as far as New Zealand to catch and sell whales.

▲ This elegant street was built in Vienna, the capital city of Austria, in the late 1700s. It is lined with many fashionable shops and cafés.

► This French political cartoon, produced at the time of the revolution (1789), shows a poor peasant weighed down by the taxes he pays to wealthy nobles and priests.

TOWN AND COUNTRY

EUROPE

In the 1700s, most people lived in the country and earned their living from the land. Rich landowners lived in stately homes. Their wealth came from the woods, fields and farms of their estates. Throughout the 1700s, enterprising landowners experimented with new farming methods, such as stock-breeding and crop rotation, to make their land more productive. Peasants lived in tumbledown cottages and grew food for their families on their own plots of land, or worked as farm labourers on the estates of the rich.

But towns and cities were growing fast. Merchants, bankers, lawyers, doctors and traders all lived there, as well as craftworkers, who made goods such as cloth, cutlery and shoes. In the biggest cities there were smart coffee shops, where men gathered to discuss business and politics, and to read the newspapers. Many seaports also became wealthy as a result of increasing international trade.

► Many towns in the Middle East were important centres of trade. This colourful picture shows crowds shopping for all kinds of bargains in the souk (covered market) in Istanbul.

A HARD LIFE

MIDDLE EAST

In many parts of the Middle East, it was hard to make a living. Dry, scorching deserts in Arabia, and high mountains and barren plains in parts of Turkey and Persia, were all unsuited to growing crops. People survived by hunting desert animals, such as gazelles and rabbits, and by raising herds of camels or breeding hardy mountain sheep and goats. In the deserts, the nomadic Bedouin people lived in tents woven from goat hair. In the mountains, villagers built well-defended houses from stone. In the marshlands of Iraq and the irrigated fields of Syria and Jordan, farmers grew a wide variety of crops. These included wheat, barley, beans, lettuce, melons and chick peas. The inhabitants of these regions built their houses from sun-dried mud brick.

FARMERS, HERDERS AND HUNTERS

African peoples at this time were either farmers, cattle-herders or hunters, depending on their environment. Farmers in the regions of present-day Zimbabwe and Tanzania grew millet and maize in the dry grasslands, while in Nigeria and Zaire, people planted crops of yams, okra and plantains in the fields cleared from the hot, damp rainforest. They carried farm produce to market towns for sale to the local rulers, merchants and craftworkers who lived there.

Nomadic cattle-herders spent their lives on the move, seeking water and grass for their animals. They lived mainly on milk, but sometimes drank fresh blood from live cattle. In the Kalahari Desert, the Khoikhoi people hunted wild animals and ate desert grubs. Close to the Cape of Good Hope, European settlers raised herds of cattle and planted maize and grapevines.

▼ This engraving shows the cattle-farming Dinka people, who lived (and still live) in the south of present-day Sudan. In the background, you can see the Dinkas' beehive-shaped homes.

SLAVERY

All around the coasts of Africa, people made a living by fishing or through trade. During the 1700s, the West African slave trade was at its height (see page 14). Under pressure from Europeans, African traders captured many people in raids. All were sold to European merchants as slaves, then shipped across the Atlantic Ocean to work in South America, the Caribbean islands and the USA. On the east coast, Arab traders also sold slaves to rich Arab and African families in Arabia, East Africa and the island of Zanzibar.

INDIAN EXPORTS

By 1700 Indian farmers and craftworkers had a long history of producing fine goods to sell. Indian silks and spices had been carried overland to Europe since ancient Greek and Roman times. But during the 1700s, many more Indians were involved in growing crops and making fabrics for export than ever before. Medicinal drugs like rhubarb and aloes (both used as laxatives) were in demand in Europe, as were spices like pepper and ginger. Indigo, a deep blue dye, was produced from plants grown on Indian farms. Indian workers grew, spun, wove and printed many types of cotton, which fetched high prices in Europe. Much of this trade was controlled by European businessmen living in Indian towns. They worked for the British East India Company, or for similar groups based in France and the Netherlands.

CROPS AND CRAFTS

Indian farmers who did not produce goods for export grew food to feed their families and to sell at markets. Indian crops varied from region to region. In the north, farmers kept cows and grew lentils and wheat. In the warmer, wetter south, they grew mangoes, coconuts and rice. Other people made useful craft items, such as leather sandals, cooking pots, carpets, furniture and bullock carts, to sell to ordinary people in India.

RICE-GROWING

Rice was the staple food crop in most of East Asia. It was grown in flooded paddy fields, where young rice seedlings were planted out in several centimetres of water. Villagers destroyed weeds by paddling barefoot in the water and stamping them into the mud. The ripe rice was harvested by hand, threshed, winnowed, polished and stored in huge pottery jars that rats and mice could not gnaw through. In colder, northern regions (north Korea and northern China), farmers grew wheat or barley instead of rice. Chilli peppers were first imported from Central America into parts of East Asia around 1700, and soon became a popular crop.

▲ This wide cotton belt, decorated with stencilled and hand-painted flowers, was made in north-west India in around 1700.

CITY LIFE

In the 1700s, most Japanese houses were made of wood. As there were frequent earthquakes in the country, the interior walls were moveable, lightweight screens made of paper and bamboo. This meant that they would not crush people inside if the houses fell down.

Japanese cities were packed with these wooden houses. Smoking was officially banned because of the risk of fire. But in fact the habit was very popular, especially in the pleasure districts known as floating worlds that were attached to big cities. There, citizens ate, drank, went to concerts and the theatre (see page 38) and watched Sumo wrestling. They also relaxed in public bath-houses, played cards and board games and enjoyed the company of beautiful, well-educated women, who were known as geishas.

◄ A Japanese audience enjoying a play in a kabuki theatre in 1745. The theatre has several stage platforms and is lit by paper lanterns.

▲ This American stately home, called Monticello, was built in the European style for the third President of the United States, Thomas Jefferson. Only the richest Americans could afford homes like this. Many ordinary farmers lived in log cabins.

EUROPEAN SETTLERS

AMERICAS

European settlers in North and South America had two main aims. These were to build new communities, run according to European political (and sometimes religious) ideas, and to make their fortunes. They cut down forests and cleared fields to create farms, where they grew maize and vegetables, planted orchards and raised chickens, pigs and cows. In the colonies of the American South, wealthier settlers ran huge plantations, where they grew tobacco, rice and cotton. Black slaves transported from West Africa, then sold to plantation owners at auctions, carried out all the heavy work in the fields. There were also enormous, European-owned estates in the Caribbean islands, where gangs of slaves harvested sugar cane and made it into sugar. It was then shipped to Europe to be sold.

NATIVE PEOPLES

Elswhere, Native peoples continued to live as they had done for thousands of years. In the high Andes Mountains of South America, peasant farmers grew potatoes and raised herds of llamas and alpacas. On the Pacific coast of Canada, fishing communities caught salmon, and harpooned seals and whales. But slowly, these lifestyles were changed through contact with Europeans. In both North and South America, Native peoples were driven from their lands when European settlers arrived and took over their fields, woods and hunting grounds. They had to adapt quickly to new, less hospitable, environments, where their old hunting, farming or fishing skills were of little use. Sometimes, they had to fight Native peoples already living in their 'new' territory, to win a share of their land.

▼ South American people harvesting corn on a settler's estate. In many parts of South America, Europeans owned the best farming land, so Native peoples had to work for them.

ISLAND LIFE

Australasia was a land of islands. The enormous continent of Australia itself was inhabited by Aboriginal peoples who followed an ancient lifestyle based on hunting and gathering wild food. But there were over 3000 smaller islands scattered across the Pacific Ocean. The peoples who lived there came from many different places and spoke hundreds of different languages. But their lives were similar. They grew sweet potatoes, yams, bananas, pumpkins, breadfruit and an edible root called taro, kept pigs, and caught fish and shellfish in coral lagoons. Most were expert sailors and travelled across the ocean using signs such as the sun, stars and clouds to navigate. They were also skilled boatbuilders and woodworkers, who made log canoes decorated with elaborate carvings.

▲ This peaceful view of the island of Tahiti, in the South Pacific Ocean, was painted by a European artist in 1792. It shows Tahitian people climbing trees to gather coconuts, and going fishing in canoes.

NEW ZEALAND

The Maori people of New Zealand lived in wooden-walled villages surrounded by vegetable gardens, where they grew kumara (an orange-fleshed sweet potato). The Maoris also gathered wild bracken roots, which they dried, ground, and boiled with water to make porridge. They hunted bats, rats, kiwis and moas – huge, flightless birds – and they made vast nets to catch eels and fish on the seashore. They also gathered seaweed and shellfish to eat, and hunted for whales. Like other Pacific islanders, the Maoris sometimes also ate the bodies of enemies captured in battle.

DISCOVERY AND INVENTION

Many people in Marie Antoinette's time devoted their lives to seeking new knowledge. Some, like British explorer Captain James Cook, travelled right around the world on their quest. Others, like American inventor Benjamin Franklin, performed dangerous experiments to investigate natural forces such as heat and electricity. Some scientists climbed mountains, or combined alarming mixtures of chemicals, to try to discover how rocks, metals and even the air we breathe were made. Others found new, more accurate ways of measuring things – from the size and shape of the universe to the passing of time.

▲ John Harrison's chronometer was a breakthrough in scientific time-keeping. No watch or clock had ever been as accurate before. Harrison designed several versions of his clock. This one was made in 1759.

NEW IDEAS

The scientific ideas of the Enlightenment (see page 41) led to a huge number of new inventions and discoveries in many parts of Europe. It was fashionable – and could be profitable – to be a scientist, doctor or engineer. Noblemen collected science books to go in their libraries. Learned societies were founded, where leading scholars gave lectures. Inventors and mechanics conducted experiments to make new materials and machines.

Some discoveries, like the coke process for smelting iron (1709), James Hargreaves' spinning jenny for mass-producing woollen thread (1767), and James Watt's steam engine (1775), helped new industries develop fast. Other discoveries were breakthroughs in understanding. For example, in 1782, Frenchman Antoine Lavoisier discovered that air is made up of the gases oxygen and nitrogen, while in 1790, Italian Luigi Galvani made progress towards discovering how electricity worked.

▲ In France during the 1700s, the Montgolfier brothers designed hot-air balloons powerful enough to lift people off the ground. The first flew near Paris in 1783.

TIME AND TEMPERATURE

Scientists in the 1700s also devised better ways of measuring time and temperature. For example, in 1718 German physicist Gabriel Fahrenheit invented the first accurate thermometer. In 1762, British clockmaker John Harrison perfected his chronometer. It enabled sailors in vast oceans, out of sight of land, to calculate their precise position.

In 1735, a new system for classifying plants and animals into different species was also developed. Swedish botanist Carolus Linnaeus showed how many seemingly different creatures (for example, cats and lions) were related, because of the way their bodies were made. His system is still used today.

◀ The spinning jenny was a machine that could spin fine, strong, even thread much faster and more cheaply than it was possible to do by hand. Machines such as this paved the way for the Industrial Revolution at the end of the 1700s.

DEADLY DISEASE

Smallpox was a highly infectious disease that spread through many countries in Marie Antoinette's time. Over half the people who caught it died. In 1719, English traveller Lady Mary Wortley Montague reported on a treatment to prevent the disease that she had seen in Istanbul. Turkish doctors took infected pus from a smallpox patient and rubbed it into scratches on healthy people's arms. Then they tied a walnut shell over the scratches, and waited for the disease to take hold. Most patients developed a mild form of smallpox, which protected them from getting the disease in future. But at least two in every hundred caught a severe form and died. After reading Lady Mary's report, European doctors copied this method of inoculation, testing it on orphans and prisoners. Then, in 1721, British king George I allowed two of his grandchildren to be inoculated. At the end of the century, British doctor Edward Jenner made inoculation safer by using pus from patients with cowpox, a similar but less dangerous disease.

ADVENTUROUS JOURNEYS

Before 1750 few Europeans had dared to travel inland in Africa. Towards the end of the century, however, two pioneering expeditions did set off. Both were led by Scotsmen inspired by scientific curiosity to explore Africa's great rivers. In 1768, James Bruce began a five-year journey through Egypt and Ethiopia to search for the source of the River Nile. In 1795, Mungo Park set off to explore the Gambia and the River Niger.

◀ Lady Mary Wortley Montague spent many years in the Middle East. Here she is shown wearing Turkish-style dress.

JAI SINGH

In India, Rajput ruler Jai Singh (died 1743) was a skilful politician and brave soldier. But he was even more respected for his scientific skills as a mathematician, astronomer, architect and town planner. Jai Singh built five huge observatories to study the stars, and sent a team of experts to meet and discuss astronomy with European scholars. He studied traditional Indian mathematics, as well as Greek and Arabic scientific writings. And he built a new capital city, Jaipur, planning its layout himself after studying many other cities in India and abroad.

▶ This dramatic engraving was made in 1860, to illustrate a copy of Mungo Park's book about his expedition of 1795. He returned to West Africa to continue exploring in 1805, but was drowned the next year.

▲ This massive observatory was built near Delhi, India, by the scholarly prince Jai Singh.

MEDICAL MARVELS

EAST ASIA

During Marie Antoinette's time, Chinese emperor Qianlong (see page 21) gave orders for all traditional Chinese medical knowledge to be collected in a huge, 40-volume encyclopedia. This was called *The Golden Mirror of Medicine*, and was completed in 1743.

For many centuries, Japanese doctors had studied Chinese medicine, and used it to treat their patients. But during the lifetime of medical reformer Goto Konzan (1659–1733), many new treatments began to be introduced. Goto believed that all disease was caused by stagnant 'life force' in the body. His new therapies were designed to get this life force flowing freely again.

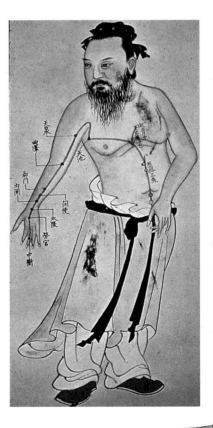

► This Chinese medical diagram, which was drawn during the 1700s, shows how to use a traditional Chinese method of healing called acupuncture to treat people suffering from heart disease.

THE BERING STRAIT

EAST ASIA

In 1728 and 1733, the Russian government gave Danish explorer Vitus Bering (1681–1741) permission to explore the Siberian coast. He mapped large areas of the coastline and explored the channel that runs between Siberia and Alaska. Today, it is still called the Bering Strait. A Russian explorer, Semyon Dezhnev, had reached Alaska in 1648, but his journey had been forgotten. Until Bering's voyages, no European scientists or governments knew that Alaska existed.

HORSE POWER

AMERICAS

Horses were introduced to the Americas from Europe in the 1500s. During the 1700s, they caused a transport revolution among Native American peoples living on the Great Plains. Horses allowed them to travel greater distances than ever before. So hunters no longer had to stay within a few days' walking distance of their homes, but could follow buffalo herds many hundreds of kilometres across the Plains. Before this time, many Plains people had lived in villages for several months each year. Horses made it possible for some to develop a nomadic lifestyle, travelling most of the time, and living in camps of easily transportable, buffalo-hide tepees.

SCIENTIFIC IDEAS

Americans whose ancestors came from Europe were interested in new European political and scientific ideas. In the 1700s they founded many libraries, colleges and schools. European scientific books were sent to America, but American scientists also made their own discoveries. Benjamin Franklin (1706–1790) carried out experiments with electricity, designed lightning conductors and ships, and invented bifocal lenses.

Other American scientists invented machines designed to help farmers. In 1793, Eli Whitney invented a cotton gin ('gin' is short for 'engine') that removed the fibres from the seed heads of the cotton plant. This made it cheaper and easier to produce cotton thread. American engineers like John Fitch and Robert Fulton experimented with designs for new, steam-powered boats.

▼ In a dangerous experiment that involved flying a kite into a thunderstorm, American politician Benjamin Franklin proved that lightning was a form of electricity.

◄ In New Zealand, Maori farmers built storehouses raised high above the ground on wooden legs to stop rats and flightless birds from stealing their crops. They decorated their homes and storehouses with beautiful carvings. This storehouse is covered with patterns showing humans fighting against bird-spirits, which were Maori symbols of life and death.

THREE EXPLORERS

From 1721 to 1722, Dutchman Jacob Roggeveen explored Samoa and the Solomon Islands. He was probably also the first European to explore mysterious Easter Island. Although the island was deserted, the colossal statues on its shores showed that it had once been home to a wealthy community. From 1766 to 1769, French scientist Louis Bougainville sailed right around the world, visiting many Pacific islands. He investigated the structure of the Earth — its rocks, mountains and volcanoes — as well as the plants and animals he saw. Between 1768 and 1779, British explorer Captain James Cook made three voyages to the region, visiting Eastern Australia, New Zealand, New Caledonia, Tonga and the Hawaiian Islands. He took specially trained artists with him to record everything of scientific interest that he observed.

PACIFIC PEOPLES

AUSTRALASIA

As the peoples of Australia, New Zealand and the Pacific kept no written records, it is difficult to find out whether they made any new inventions or discoveries during the 1700s. But European travellers who met them reported that they had many ingenious ways of farming, hunting and fishing, and that they built fine houses and canoes. Europeans also described the traditional customs of the Pacific peoples. Some of these, such as cannibalism, horrified them. Others, like bravery and hospitality, they very much admired.

► This scorpion fish from the Pacific Ocean was painted by Sydney Parkinson, one of the artists who accompanied Captain Cook on his first scientific voyage around the world, from 1768 to 1771. As well as paintings like this, Cook brought home shells, bones, fossils and many plant specimens.

THE CREATIVE WORLD

In Marie Antoinette's time, the arts – painting, sculpture, architecture, music, dance and theatre – were designed to impress. Palaces, paintings, statues, plays, concerts and operas were all meant to show their creators' skill and the wealth and good taste of the kings, queens and other powerful people who paid vast sums for them. Far from the stately homes and big cities, among ordinary people, the arts had many other purposes. They formed part of important ceremonies and events, such as marriages, funerals, farming festivals and even preparations for warfare. Growing naturally out of everyday life, they bound people and communities together.

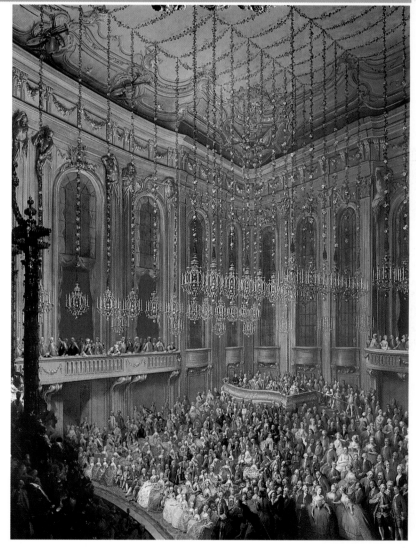

▲ A gala concert celebrating a royal wedding in the palace of Empress Maria Theresa. The audience are listening to the young musician and composer Wolfgang Amadeus Mozart, aged five, playing the harpsichord.

◄ This bronze disc commemorates the founding of St Petersburg by Tsar (Emperor) Peter the Great in 1703.

PRECIOUS TREASURES

MIDDLE EAST

Powerful Middle Eastern rulers paid for top artists and craftspeople to produce wonderful works of art for their palaces. The Ottoman emperors of Turkey collected silk carpets, painted ceramics, gold and silver dishes and glittering swords encrusted with rubies and diamonds. When Persian ruler Nadir Shah invaded India in 1739, he seized the world's most famous diamond – the massive Koh-i-Noor (Mountain of Light) – to add to his royal treasury.

ART FOR RICH AND POOR

EUROPE

During the 1700s, some of Europe's grandest palaces, including Schönbrunn in Austria and Buckingham Palace in England, were built. Elegant new towns, such as Williamsburg in the USA, Bath in England and St Petersburg in Russia, were also constructed. Artists like Frenchwoman Elisabeth Vigée-Lebrun and Englishman Sir Joshua Reynolds painted stylish portraits, while Frenchman Antoine Watteau and Englishman Thomas Gainsborough painted beautiful landscapes. In Austria and Hungary, composers Wolfgang Amadeus Mozart and Franz Josef Haydn wrote brilliant music. German composer Georg Frederik Handel moved to England, where he wrote operas, and also *Messiah*, a famous choral work.

The arts admired by the wealthy few were not available to ordinary people. They could not enter the picture galleries and music rooms of grand houses. They could not afford books, or tickets to operas and plays. Instead, they enjoyed folk songs, country dances, ballads and rude cartoons that mocked the rich and powerful.

COLOURFUL COSTUMES

Ordinary people in the Middle East embroidered their clothes using wool or cotton coloured with vegetable dyes. Some women wore headdresses and necklaces of silver coins. In country areas with no banks, this was the best way to look after their savings. Nomadic peoples also decorated their tents, carpets, even the saddlebags of horses and camels, with elaborate geometric designs.

▼ An Ottoman royal hunting party in the 1700s. The sultan, in the centre, is seated on a rich carpet and embroidered cushions.

BRASS FROM BENIN

In West Africa, highly skilled brassworkers from the kingdom of Benin made portrait heads of important people, and brass plaques that recorded traditional stories and important events. These were used to decorate the palace of the oba (king) in the centre of the city of Benin. In the nearby Asanti kingdom, metalworkers made hundreds of tiny brass weights. These were used for weighing gold dust, the Asanti people's chief wealth. In Central and Southern Africa, some of the best craftworkers and artists made religious carvings and masks, or clothes and jewellery.

◀ The Asanti made brass weights in the shape of everyday objects, like this man on a horse. Sometimes the weights were decorated with magical or holy patterns, too.

INDIAN MINIATURES

By 1700 there was already a long tradition of painting miniatures in India. These were tiny, very precise paintings in glowing colours and full of fascinating details. Often, they were decorated with an ornate border. Many were designed to be pasted into albums, where they could be kept safe and admired. Elsewhere in South Asia, craftworkers produced fine textiles and metalwork. On the Indonesian islands of Java and Bali, most men carried a type of dagger called a kris. If they could afford it, they had the handle decorated with elaborate designs.

KABUKI CULTURE

EAST ASIA

In Japan, kabuki theatre was one of the most popular art forms. It had been invented in about 1603 by a woman entertainer called Okuni, but by the 1700s was performed only by men. Kabuki plays were exciting, with lots of action, elaborate costumes and special effects using revolving stages and trapdoors. Kabuki actors sang and danced, as well as speaking. They were accompanied by an on-stage orchestra. (You can see one on page 27.) Many traditional stories were used as plots for plays. But in the 1700s, dramatist Tsuruya Nambku IV created the first kabuki 'gangster' plays, about thieves and murderers. Audiences loved them!

▼ This Indian miniature, painted in around 1770, shows a princess in a beautiful garden, surrounded by peacocks. She is carrying a lute.

◀ This painting, in 'Primitive' American settler style, shows people and animals living together in an imaginary world. Pictures like this reflected the settlers' wish to build a godly and peaceful kingdom in their new homeland.

TRADITION AND CHANGE

AMERICAS

By the 1700s, Native Americans living in both the north and south of the continent had been making art objects for hundreds of years. They ranged from massive stone temples to fragile pottery and delicate jewels. Each nation had its own artistic styles. Many of these traditions continued throughout the 1700s, but others changed under the influence of new materials, techniques and designs brought by Europeans who had settled in American lands.

OLD STONE, NEW BEADS

In South America and the southern USA, Christian missionaries built many churches and monasteries. Sometimes they used the stones of earlier non-Christian temples for their new buildings. In North America, European traders sold brightly-coloured glass beads to Native American women living in the north-east and on the Great Plains. The women used these beads to decorate clothes, belts, shoes and headdresses. They were longer-lasting, easier to sew and much quicker to obtain than the porcupine quills that had traditionally been used for these items.

SETTLER STYLES

European settler artists and craftworkers developed their own new styles and techniques. American 'Primitive' artists created paintings in a deliberately plain style that was influenced by their simple lifestyle and forms of religious worship. In remote country districts there were no shops, so settler women often had to recycle material. They created beautiful patchwork quilts from old scraps of cloth.

PACIFIC ARTS

AUSTRALASIA

When the first European explorers reached the Pacific islands, they were fascinated by the arts and crafts of the local peoples. European travellers recorded seeing tattoos and body paintings in graceful, swirling designs, sculptures of gods and goddesses made from shells, sharks' teeth, wood and stone, and carved doorways on the houses of chiefs.

In Australia, Aboriginal artists continued their ancient traditions of cave painting and rock engraving. Another important art form was the telling of traditional stories, often through dance and song. In this way, elders passed on the history of their people, as well as their ideas and beliefs.

BELIEFS AND IDEAS

Are old ideas always right? Should people always value ancient beliefs or be prepared to replace them? Do scientific laws or mysterious forces control the world? Are calm discussions or dramatic revolutions the best way to bring about change? All these questions – and many more – faced people during the 1700s. Suddenly, new scientific discoveries and political ideas were challenging the views held by rulers, scholars and religious leaders for centuries. In many different parts of the world, important people responded to these challenges in many different ways. Some strengthened their traditional beliefs and ideas. Others hurried to accept the new.

▲ In 1766, British artist and scientist Joseph Wright of Derby painted this dramatic picture of an astronomer and his family with an orrery – a model of the Earth, Sun, Moon and planets.

CHRISTIAN BELIEFS

In Europe during the 1700s, most people called themselves Christians. But there were many varieties of the Christian faith. Marie Antoinette, her family in Austria, and most of the people she ruled in France were Roman Catholics. Most Spanish and Italian people were Catholics, too. But in England, Germany and Scandinavia, the majority of people were Protestants. They disagreed with some Roman Catholic beliefs and ways of worship.

JOHN WESLEY

By 1700, new religious movements were calling for church reforms. John Wesley (1703–1791) was a Protestant priest and university teacher in England. He became leader of a group of Christians nicknamed 'Methodists'.

Wesley encouraged ordinary people to worship in a direct and simple way. He travelled around Britain preaching in the open air, founded Methodist chapels, wrote books on religion and composed rousing hymns. His preaching alarmed the Church of England authorities, but attracted many followers.

◀ The sermons of preacher John Wesley appealed to ordinary people who did not normally go to church.

▶ A decorated copy of the Qur'an. Muslim reformers in the 1700s wanted people to concentrate on the meaning of the Qur'an's holy words rather than on admiring beautiful pages like these.

THE ENLIGHTENMENT

At the same time as the Methodists were winning support, traditional Christianity in Europe was being challenged by a new movement based on scientific, deliberately non-religious ideas. Members of this movement, known as the Enlightenment, sought the truth by relying only on human intelligence, not religious beliefs. The movement was strongest in France and Germany, but there were supporters elsewhere in Europe. Members believed that their search for truth would improve everyone's lives. French thinker Jean Jacques Rousseau planned new forms of education designed to teach people to live simply and honestly. In 1777, Frenchman Denis Diderot completed a 33-volume encyclopedia, containing all the latest Enlightenment discoveries and ideas.

ISLAMIC IDEAS

During the 1700s, most people in the Middle East were Muslims. Muhammad ibn Abd al-Wahhab (1703–1792) wanted them to return to older, purer ways of worship. In his Book of Unity, he called for worship to be based only on the Qur'an, the Muslim holy book, and for governments to base their laws on sharia, the Muslim holy law.

BAAL SHEM TOV

Jewish leader Baal Shem Tov (1700–1760) distrusted the form of Judaism taught by the top scholars of his day. He called for Jewish people to return to the basis of their religion – total devotion to God. He taught them to worship God simply, through eager prayers and joyful singing and dancing, and to oppose the scholars' reforms. Baal Shem Tov's ideas became popular among poor people in country areas of Eastern Europe and the Middle East. Later, they developed into a branch of Judaism called Hasidism, which still exists today.

HOLY WAR

In North Africa, many people were Muslims. There were also centres of Islamic learning in the region, such as the cities of Djenne and Timbuktu. But many African Muslims lived in countries where the laws and customs were based on traditional, non-Muslim beliefs. During the 1700s, leaders such as Usman dan Fodio (1754–1817) called for the purification of African Islam. He finally led a jihad (holy war) against the rulers of northern Nigeria. Once they were defeated, he set up a new kingdom modelled on the first Muslim empire and governed by religious laws based on the Qur'an.

TRADITIONAL BELIEFS

In the rest of Africa, people continued to follow traditional beliefs. These included honouring their dead ancestors, and making offerings of food and objects to the magical spirits, gods and goddesses who were believed to watch over different aspects of life. For example, in the West African kingdom of Benin, women made offerings at little shrines dedicated to Olokun, the god of fertility, wealth and good fortune. To protect their families, they made shrines to the god Esu outside their homes. They believed Esu would drive away evil.

▲ A Jewish marriage contract from the 1700s. Baal Shem Tov wanted religion to play a part in every stage of life.

HINDU WORSHIP

Although large areas of India were ruled by Muslim Mughal emperors, the majority of the population were Hindus. There were also communities of Buddhists, Muslims, Sikhs, Jains and Parsees. Hinduism was a very ancient faith. Over the centuries, many styles of Hindu worship had developed. In the 1700s, a way of worshipping called Bhakti was popular. It encouraged ordinary Hindus to take a direct part in religious ceremonies, rather than leaving prayers and rituals to scholars, holy men and priests. Ordinary people joined in prayers, processions and pilgrimages. They sang religious songs using everyday language rather than ancient Sanskrit, which few understood.

As British power in India grew, British people began to criticize Hinduism. This led to mistrust between Britons and Indians of many faiths.

▲ The Golden Temple at Amritsar, India, is the Sikhs' most important religious centre. The temple holds the *Granth Sahib*, the Sikhs' holy book. When Guru Gobind Singh died, he said that there would be no more gurus. Instead he told people to read the *Granth Sahib* for guidance.

▼ Villagers worshipping Hindu gods at a holy place in the Himalaya Mountains. This picture was painted by a European in about 1800.

SIKH WARRIORS

The Sikh religion was founded in the Punjab region of northern India around 1500. During the 1700s, Sikh warriors fought to protect their faith. They were led by Guru Gobind Singh (died 1708) and Prince Ranjit Singh (1780–1839). Guru Gobind Singh, the last of the Sikhs' Great Gurus (religious leaders), battled against persecution by Mughal emperors. Ranjit Singh struggled to achieve independence for Sikh lands.

CLOSED COUNTRIES

EAST ASIA

Throughout the 1700s, China and Japan were both almost entirely cut off from contact with the other nations of the world (see page 16). This was their rulers' own decision. They thought of all outsiders, and particularly Europeans, as 'foreign devils', and they did not want them to spread alien ideas and religions, such as Christianity, among their people.

▲ This temple in the city of Qufu, China, was built to honour the ancient philosopher Confucius.

RELIGIOUS BELIEFS

EAST ASIA

For Chinese and Japanese rulers, and for many ordinary Chinese and Japanese people as well, their religion was linked to their sense of national pride. Most Chinese people followed the teachings of Confucius, a philosopher who lived in around 500 BC. He taught people to honour their parents and teachers, and to treat one another with respect. On the emperor's orders, the temple at Confucius's birthplace at Qufu in the state of Lu was rebuilt in 1724.

In Japan, Shinto was the most widespread religion. It was based on the worship of sacred spirits. They were believed to be all around – in the souls of great leaders, in gods and goddesses, in holy places such as Mount Fuji, and even in rocks, lakes, rivers and streams.

SHARED IDEAS

AMERICAS

Each Native American people had its own holy myths and legends, religious faith and ways of worship. But almost all their religions had ideas in common. They all shared a belief in Mother Earth, and a reverence for all living things. They all believed that sacrifices, and sometimes suffering, might persuade the gods and spirits to help them. They also believed that priests and healers called shamans had the power to communicate with the spirits, through prayers, meditation, music and dancing. People hoped that the shamans' skills would bring them good fortune in their lives, or at least drive away bad luck.

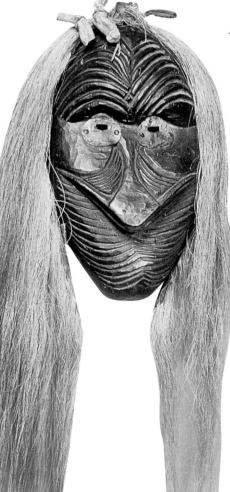

◄ Native peoples from north-east America made masks from carved wood and animal hair to wear at special religious ceremonies. These were thought to protect people and their homes from harm, and to heal sickness.

THE DELAWARE PROPHET

During the 1700s, several Native American shamans felt inspired to lead their people against the European settlers. For example, the Delaware Prophet (his real name is unknown) began to preach to peoples in north-east America in about 1762. He said that he had received a vision of a glorious new future. If Native Americans returned to their traditional ways of life, gave up their guns and everything else they had purchased or copied from Europeans, they would grow strong again. This would enable them to drive the foreigners from their lands. A few powerful Native American leaders, for example Pontiac (see page 23), followed some of the Delaware Prophet's advice. But, tragically, the glorious new future he had promised never arrived.

▲ Pacific islanders, like these men from Hawaii, made offerings to gods and spirits. This was a way of asking for their help and protection.

SUPERNATURAL POWER

In many parts of the Pacific, kings and chiefs relied on supernatural power, which they called mana, to help them rule. They and their subjects believed that mana was given by the gods to certain chosen people, as a reward for goodness, bravery or wisdom. A ruler who had mana won extra respect, because it would help him to achieve success in wars or to govern his people well. Mana could also belong to objects, such as statues of the gods, or to holy places, where powerful spirits were worshipped.

PEOPLES FROM AROUND THE WORLD

Aboriginals The first inhabitants of Australia, who arrived there about 40,000 years ago.

Asanti Farmers, traders and skilled metalworkers who lived in the region of present-day Ghana.

Bambara Warriors and cattle herders who lived in the region of present-day Mali.

Bini (also called Edo) Farmers and traders who lived in the kingdom of Benin, in the region of present-day Nigeria.

Buganda (also called Ganda) Farmers and hunters who lived in the region of present-day Uganda.

Dinka Nomadic cattle-herders who lived in the region of present-day southern Sudan and in the Rift Valley area to the south.

Fulani Cattle-herders and town-builders who lived in the region of present-day Chad, Senegal and western Sudan.

Hausa Farmers, craftworkers and traders who lived in the region of present-day north and central Nigeria.

Khoikhoi Nomadic hunters and gatherers who lived in south-western Africa.

Kirghiz Semi-nomadic farmers who raised sheep and goats in wild regions of Central Asia.

Luanda (also called Mbundu) Farmers and hunters who lived in the region of present-day Angola and nearby lands.

Maoris Settlers in New Zealand who arrived there from the Pacific Islands in about 800 AD.

Marathas A powerful people, led by warrior princes, who lived in central India.

Masai Cattle-herders and hunters who lived in and around the region of present-day Kenya.

Mons Rice farmers who lived in the region of present-day Thailand and Burma.

Native Americans The first inhabitants of America, who arrived there about 30,000 years ago. Native American people were divided into many nations.

Ottawa Native American peoples who lived as traders, hunters and farmers in eastern Canada.

Seneca Native American peoples who lived as hunters and farmers in the region of present-day New York State, USA.

Xhosa Cattle farmers who lived in the region of present-day Transkei, South Africa.

Yoruba Farmers and traders who lived in the region of present-day Nigeria and Benin.

acupuncture A system of Chinese medicine that aims to cure illness by placing needles under the skin to balance forces within the body.
alliance A friendly agreement between nations.
auction A sale in which buyers make bids (offers of money) for goods. The highest bid wins.

ballad A song that tells a story.
bamboo A plant that looks rather like giant grass. Its stems and leaves are used for building.
bifocal lenses Specially shaped pieces of glass used in spectacles. They allow wearers to see both close and distant objects.
breadfruit A large, round, heavy tropical fruit with starchy flesh.
bureaucracy A system of government that relies on large numbers of well-trained officials to collect taxes and enforce laws.

cannibalism The eating of people by other people, often as part of religious ceremonies.
cavalry Soldiers on horseback.
ceramics Beautiful objects – pots, tiles and statues – made of clay.
chapel A small Christian church.
choral work A piece of music performed by many people singing together in a choir.
city-state A city that also rules the surrounding countryside.
civil war Fighting between groups in the same country.
colonize To take over and rule a weaker country.

colony A country that has been colonized (see above).

confederation An alliance (see above) between a group of friendly, equal nations or peoples.

constitution A set of rules and laws for running a country.

crop rotation Changing the crops grown in fields each year, to stop the build-up of pests and to allow the soil to regain its goodness.

dynasty A ruling family.

empire A large area of land, including several different nations or peoples, that is governed by a single ruler called an emperor.

engraving A picture produced by printing from an image cut into a wooden block or metal plate.

estate A large area of land owned by a single family.

fossil The remains of a living creature millions of years old that have been turned to stone.

Holy Roman Emperor An ancient title belonging to a European royal family. It was abolished in 1806.

Industrial Revolution The time (from around 1750 to 1900) of change in northern Europe and North America in which steam power and new machines were invented, new factories and towns were built, and new forms of transport developed.

inoculation A way of protecting people against serious disease by deliberately infecting them with a milder form of the same illness.

irrigation Channelling water to dry land so crops can grow there.

kimono A long, loose coat with wide sleeves worn in Japan.

lightning conductor A metal strip fixed to tall buildings to carry the electricity from lightning safely down to the ground.

meditation Thinking deeply about spiritual things.

millet A food crop that is related to rice and other grains.

missionary A person who travels to another country to spread their religious beliefs.

monastery A religious community where monks and nuns live apart from the world.

Mother Earth The earth viewed as a goddess who feeds and provides for her people.

musket A type of gun.

navigation The skill and science of steering a course at sea.

nomadic Moving from place to place in search of food or of grazing land for animals.

okra A vegetable that has small, edible pods with soft flesh.

philosopher A person who studies knowledge and wisdom.

pilgrimage A special journey to visit a holy place.

plantain A green, banana-like fruit cooked as a vegetable.

plantation An area of land where one crop, such as sugar, is grown.

plaque A piece of carved metal or stone, usually fixed to a wall.

reform A change that aims to improve something.

regent A person who rules on behalf of a king or queen.

regiment A group of soldiers.

republic A country ruled by elected leaders, not a monarch.

savannah Dry grassland.

smelt To crush then heat rocks containing metal until the metal melts and runs out.

stock-breeding A way of improving farm animals, such as cows, by breeding only the fittest.

Sumo wrestling A popular Japanese sport perfomed by very large, strong wrestlers.

sweet potato A yellow-fleshed fruit cooked as a vegetable.

taboo Having special powers, either for good or bad. The idea of 'taboo' forms part of the religious beliefs of many Pacific islanders.

taro A fleshy root crop cooked as a vegetable.

tepee An animal-skin tent made by some Native Americans.

thresh To separate grains and seeds from plant stalks, usually by hitting them with a large stick.

treason The crime of betraying one's country or ruler.

tribute Money or goods paid to rulers or governments.

warlord A warrior leader who controls parts of a country.

winnow To separate grains and seeds from their casing, often by throwing them up into the air.

yam A root crop that is cooked and eaten as a vegetable.